DON'T I

MW01614001

By
EDDIE ZIPPERER

Dramatic Publishing
Woodstock, Illinois • England • Australia • New Zealand

*** NOTICE ***

IMPORTANT BILLING AND CREDIT REQUIREMENTS

All producers of the play *must* give credit to the author of the play in all programs distributed in connection with performances of the play and in all instances in which the title of the play appears for purposes of advertising, publicizing or otherwise exploiting the play and/or a production. The name of the author *must* also appear on a separate line, on which no other name appears, immediately following the title, and *must* appear in size of type not less than fifty percent (50%) the size of the title type. Biographical information on the author, if included in the playbook, may be used in all programs. *In all programs this notice must appear:*

Don't Fear the Reaper's first scene was originally produced as a ten-minute play entitled *The Doorstep* at Georgia State College & University's (Milledgeville) 24-Hour Plays with the following artists:

Director . . . . Brian Jones

Robert . . . . Conan Joshua Santamaria
Jessica . . . . Elisha Hodgin
Death . . . . Warren Downs
Jack. . . . . Peter Springsted

The show in its entirety was originally produced at Augusta Preparatory Day School in 2008 with the following artists:

Director . . . . Jamie M. McAteer

Death/Bill . . . . Michael Sodomka
Robert/Jeremy/Announcer . . . . Adam Kronowski
Jessica. . . . . Kirsten Newlin
Donnie Destiny/Jack . . . . John Duggan
Steve . . . . Stuart Lee
God. . . . . Yutong Dong
Satan . . . . Samantha K. Osburn
Conception . . . . Alex Ploetzke
Game Show Crew . . . . Adam Kronowski & Alex Ploetzke

Lights & Sound. William Bailey
Lights . . . . Deema Elchoufi

DON'T FEAR THE REAPER

CHARACTERS

DEATH (BILL) . . . . . the Grim Reaper in his classic form
ROBERT . . . . a 30-year-old grocery store manager
JESSICA . . . . a 30-year-old housewife
JACK . . . . a dead man
STEVE . . a lazy young man who is a gamer and television
connoisseur
GOD . . . . King of Kings
SATAN . . . . a beautiful, seductive woman
JEREMY . . . . the Grim Reaper of insects
CONCEPTION . . . . the opposite of Death; his wife
DONNIE DESTINY . . . . a game show host
ANNOUNCER. . . . . a game show announcer
TWO GAME SHOW CREW MEMBERS

PLACE: Three suburban living rooms and God's office.

TIME: The present.

5

DON'T FEAR THE REAPER

SCENE ONE

SETTING: *A living room located somewhere in suburbia. There is a sofa in the room and the front door of the house is located upstage.*

AT RISE: *ROBERT enters. He has long hair, but it is pulled up into a ponytail. He looks clean-cut. His wife, JESSICA, yells to him from offstage.*

JESSICA *(from offstage)*. Robert, you forgot your keys!

ROBERT. I don't need them. Jack is picking me up today. We have a meeting with the regional managers at 8:30. *(He looks at his watch.)* A meeting that we're going to be late for if he doesn't hurry. *(ROBERT plops on the sofa and begins looking around.)* Do you know where the remote control is?

JESSICA *(offstage)*. Wherever you put it.

ROBERT. Damn it! I wanted to check out Sportscenter to see if the Sox won.

JESSICA. Since when do you care about baseball?

ROBERT. I don't, but the guys I'm meeting with do. It's important to be able to talk to these guys. That's how you sell yourself. They're always saying crap like, "Can you believe Johnson got hurt? He's going on the L.D," or "Did you see such and such pitcher hit that home run last night?"

JESSICA *(peeks her head in)*. Pitchers don't hit in the American League, honey. Why don't you bring in the paper and read the sports page?

ROBERT. Oh yeah.

(ROBERT opens the door. DEATH, in all his pale, skeletal black-hooded glory, is on the other side of the door. ROBERT and DEATH stare at each other for a long moment. Finally, ROBERT calmly closes the door and begins to take off his tie.)

ROBERT. I think I'm going to stay home today.

(He is visibly worried. He begins pacing. JESSICA enters wearing an apron.)

JESSICA. Did you say you're staying home today? You can't stay home today. Are you sick?

ROBERT. No, I'm not sick at all! Are you sick?

JESSICA. No. Why would I be sick?

ROBERT. I've never felt better in my life! Let me feel your pulse.

JESSICA. What? You're worrying me, Robert. Your face is turning all white.

ROBERT *(distracted)*. Yeah. Maybe I should go lay down or something. *(JESSICA goes back in the other room. ROBERT walks to the front door.)* I'm not sick though!

JESSICA *(offstage)*. Okay!

ROBERT *(to DEATH)*. Look, I'm not ready to go yet. One more year. Okay. One more year. I have a lot of important things going on right now. Especially at work. I'm chipping away at this promotion—you can't take me before I get the promotion. I've been kissing my boss' fat ass for five years to get this promotion. I earned it. At least give me that. I'm sure you hear this all the time, but I'm about to be made head manager of the organic foods store I work for, and I think I'm gonna be really good at it. One of the bag boys told me the other day that if he were a manager, he'd be a cool one like me. Anyway, it's not the most impressive job, but I take pride in it. Let me do that for a little bit, and then I'll go. I won't say a word. I'll go quietly. Six more months, okay. Six more months? *(He peeks out the window.)* Damn it. Why won't you leave?

(JESSICA enters.)

JESSICA. I thought you were getting back in bed.

(ROBERT sits down on the sofa.)

ROBERT. No. I'm just going to sit in here for a while.
JESSICA. You want me to help you find the remote?
ROBERT. No. I watch too much TV.
JESSICA. Now I know you're sick.
ROBERT. I think I'll just read the paper. *(JESSICA goes back to the kitchen. ROBERT sits for a moment trying to think. He has an idea.)* Hey, Jessica!
JESSICA *(offstage)*. Yeah?
ROBERT. I think I do feel a little sick. Will you go get the paper for me?
JESSICA *(offstage)*. I'm busy cooking dinner.

ROBERT. Dinner? It's 8:00 in the morning.

JESSICA *(offstage)*. Yes. It takes all day to make a turkey.

ROBERT. It'll only take you five seconds. It's right on the doorstep.

JESSICA *(offstage)*. I told you, I'm busy.

ROBERT. You weren't busy ten seconds ago when you came in here!

JESSICA *(offstage)*. I had a break. Now I'm busy again.

ROBERT. Okay. I'm gonna go lay down. When you see Jack drive up, will you go out and tell him that I'm sick?

JESSICA *(offstage)*. Why can't you?

ROBERT *(peeks out the window again)*. Because I'm not sick, and I don't look sick. I'm the living portrait of a very, very healthy man, and why wouldn't I be? I'm only thirty for God's sake. Besides, I'm getting back in bed.

JESSICA *(offstage)*. I think I see his car coming down the street right now. Just run out and tell him.

ROBERT. Please, Jessica. It'll take five seconds. Just run out there, tell him I'm sick, run right back in. That turkey's not going to miraculously spring back to life, pop out a new head, and fly away because you turn your back for five little seconds, is it?

JESSICA *(offstage)*. I can't right now, Robert!

ROBERT. Fine! I'll call him! God! *(ROBERT takes out his cell phone and dials as he walks downstage. In a sickly voice:)* Jack, this is Robert. *(Coughs.)* Look, I'm not going to be able to make it to the meeting this morning. I'm really sick. *(Coughs harder.)* I'm really sorry. I owe you one. I'll come in early Friday morning and open the store for you. Good luck with the meeting.

(ROBERT hangs up. JESSICA enters.)

JESSICA. Did you get it taken care of?

ROBERT. Yes. I left him a voice mail. I thought you were busy.

JESSICA. I had another break, and I wanted to check on you. You're acting really weird.

ROBERT. It's hot as hell in here! Will you pull that door open? *(ROBERT takes a step back.)*

JESSICA. I don't want the door open. I'm already cold, and it's freezing out there this morning. You're just feeling hot because you have a fever. Why don't you sit out on the doorstep until your temperature gets back down to normal. That's how you cool down.

ROBERT. I guess you're right. It is a little chilly in here. I'll just turn up the heat. *(ROBERT adjusts the thermostat.)*

JESSICA. Be careful. What did you set it on?

ROBERT. One-o-five. That'll warm you up. Yep, it's gonna be like a sauna in here soon.

JESSICA. That's fine with me. Whatever makes you feel better, sweetie. Now, go lay down.

(ROBERT exits. JESSICA runs over to the door and speaks to DEATH.)

JESSICA. I don't know which one of us you're here for, but Robert is two years older than me. Did you know that? It's not fair. I haven't gotten to do anything with my life yet. He spends every day meeting new people and having interesting conversations with all the neighbors who shop at Natural Mart. Who do I get to talk to?

Nobody, that's who! *(JESSICA sits down on the floor next to the door with her knees pulled up to her chest.)* My whole life isn't any different than this morning, really. A prisoner in this house, knowing that death is lurking and I haven't accomplished anything at all. I know that we're all insignificant in the grand scheme of things, but I'm still insignificant in the small scheme. Just wait for me to do one meaningful thing, please. Just let me make my tiny little insignificant life matter to one person. Then, I'm yours.

(ROBERT enters in his boxers, walks to the thermostat and begins messing with it. JESSICA gets up quickly and walks toward him.)

ROBERT. Would you believe this thermostat goes up to 120 degrees? That's perfect.

JESSICA. You're setting it on 120?

ROBERT. If it's too hot for you, you can always step outside.

JESSICA. Not at all. I said I was cold, didn't I?

ROBERT. Good.

JESSICA. Good.

(JESSICA exits. ROBERT runs over to the door.)

ROBERT *(to DEATH)*. I'm through bargaining. You should know that I have a gun in here. I guess I can't kill you with it since you're Death, or whatever, but it will at least mess you up. It's not a pansy .22 either. My dad was a weapons collector before you took him. That's right, and he left all that crap to me. I have an arsenal five steps away from me, and I won't hesitate to blow those rotten old bones to dust!

(JESSICA enters in something skimpy. ROBERT stands up.)

JESSICA. Bring on the heat.

(They both sit on the sofa. They are silent for a few seconds.)

ROBERT. I wonder if it's 120 yet.

JESSICA. Doesn't feel like it to me.

ROBERT. Well, it will be soon. Yep. It's gonna get sweaty in here. Hair sticking to your face, clothes sticking to your body. But at least you're still safe. It's when you stop sweating that you have to worry. You start getting headaches, feeling dizzy. That's when you know heatstroke is setting in.

JESSICA. You've got a good fifty pounds on me, so let me know when you start feeling it. It doesn't bother me. Not one bit.

ROBERT. Me either. *(They sit in silence with their arms crossed for a few seconds. ROBERT sighs extremely loud.)* I sure wouldn't mind having that newspaper right now.

JESSICA. Fine, Robert! If you want the newspaper that much, then I'll go get it for you. *(She takes one step toward the door then turns.)* Just like I do everything else for you. *(She takes another step toward the door then turns again.)* Just like I cook your dinners, and clean your house, and watch whatever you choose on TV because you had a hard day. *(She steps toward the door then turns again.)* I have hard days too, Robert, but I don't complain. *(She steps toward the door then turns again.)* I don't complain because I just want you to be happy. That's all. I just thought you should know that before I get the paper.

(ROBERT watches as JESSICA slowly grabs the doorknob.)

ROBERT. Wait!

JESSICA. What?

ROBERT. Never mind. *(She grabs the doorknob again. She almost begins to open it.)* No, wait! *(ROBERT jumps up and stops her.)* I'm the one who wants to read the paper. I should be the one to get it. I'm sorry I tried to make you get it.

JESSICA. Why can't we just say screw the paper? Let a hundred of them pile up out there, and just stay in this living room forever? I don't want either of us to get the paper.

ROBERT. We have to accept it, Jessica. Let's come out and say it. We both know that Death is on our doorstep, and he's not leaving here without one of us. *(Pause.)* I'll go.

JESSICA. No, I—

ROBERT. Shhh. It's okay. I'm sorry that I tried to send you out there. I wouldn't really have let you go, you know? I want you to have a good life, Jessica. That's all I've ever wanted for you. I wish I could have given you everything that you deserved, but the present was for work and money and responsibility, and it was exhausting. Tomorrows were for all the good stuff, and you start to feel like they'll never run out, but I guess mine finally have. Goodbye, Jessica. *(He kisses her. He starts to open the door.)* One more thing.

JESSICA. What is it?

ROBERT. There's a flash drive for the computer in the pocket of my pants. I told a friend I would hold onto it for him, so if it has pornography on it or something, it's his. Not mine.

JESSICA. Okay. *(ROBERT slowly starts to open the door.)* Stop. *(He stops.)* Why should we just give in like this? That's exactly what's wrong with us. We just give in to people and let them push us around. So what, Death shows up, and he just gets to take us? The stakes are too high to just give up and die. Everyone has to go, but nobody has to go quietly.

ROBERT. Yeah. Yeah. We're Americans! It's our right— screw that—it's our duty to stand up to this guy and say, "you can take our lives if that's your job, but you're going to have to earn your payday just like everyone else in this country!" Let's do it then. *(ROBERT exits and reenters with a machine gun and ammo strapped over his shoulder. He steps up onto the couch.)* Get behind me. *(JESSICA gets behind him. ROBERT takes the rubber band out and lets his hair down. They strike a pose that belongs on the cover of a romance novel.)* All right, Death! You want us? You come in here and take us! You hear me, you sick sack of bones? We built this life with our blood, sweat and tears, and I'll damn well defend it with them too. You've got to the count of three to get in here, or I'm gonna come out there, and you don't want me to come out there, pal! One! Two! *(Long pause.)* Three!

(ROBERT creeps to the door with JESSICA behind him. He pauses for a moment and then pulls it open quickly. A large man is lying dead on the doorstep. DEATH is gone.)

JESSICA. Oh my God. Who is it?

ROBERT *(bends down and checks the guy's pulse)*. It's Jack. He was here for Jack. After all that nonsense and bickering, he wasn't here for either of us.

JESSICA. Poor Jack. I wonder how long he's been there?

ROBERT. I don't know, but it's freezing out here. *(ROBERT shuts the door.)* I guess this means that you're stuck with me for at least one more day.

JESSICA. You're not so bad. *(They hug.)* The weird thing is, now that it's ended well, not for Jack but for us, I think this was the best day of my life.

ROBERT. Yeah, I know what you mean.

JESSICA. What do we do now?

(There is a short pause.)

ROBERT. Let's find the remote.

(Blackout.)

SCENE TWO

SETTING: *The living room is changed around to become a different living room.*

AT RISE: *STEVE, a young man who appears to be a bit of a slob, is sitting on the couch asleep. There is a bag of chips on the floor next to him and lots of crumbs on him. It is obvious that he lives in front of the television. DEATH enters. He is the classical embodiment of death, black, hooded cloak and extremely pale. He stops and stares at STEVE. He pokes him with his scythe.*

STEVE *(still asleep).* Wha—?

(He slaps at the spot where he was poked. When DEATH speaks, his voice is very deep and foreboding.)

DEATH. It is time to come with me, Steve. You have reached the ultimate fork in the river of your life.

STEVE *(still asleep).* Five more minutes.

DEATH. Steve. Wake up, Steve. *(He pokes him harder.)*

STEVE *(still asleep, but closer to waking).* Just five more mintues, Grandma.

DEATH. I'm not your grandma, Steve. I am the Omega. I am...death. *(He waits a moment for a reaction, then pokes STEVE again.)* Seriously, Steve, you have to get up now.

STEVE. All right. *(Sits up and rubs his eyes.)* It's not even noon yet. Why do I— *(He sees DEATH, screams, and jumps up.)* What!? Who? You're—

DEATH. Yes, Steve. I am the Omega. I am...Death.

STEVE *(looks around).* Grandma's not home.

DEATH. I'm not here for Grandma.

STEVE. Oh. Well, Grandpa's already dead.

DEATH. I'm not here for Grandpa either.

STEVE. Oh. Who are you here for?

DEATH. I'm here for you. You died five minutes ago.

(STEVE looks at where he was sitting on the couch. A few moments pass.)

STEVE *(mournfully)*. What happened to me? Heart attack? An aneurysm? That's what took my dad.

DEATH. No, Steve, you fell asleep with chips in your mouth.

STEVE. I guess I was pretty tired.

DEATH. Not really.

STEVE. Oh.

DEATH. It's called sloth, Steve, and it's one of the deadly sins.

STEVE. I can't believe this is happening. I was going to go to college.

DEATH. No you weren't.

STEVE. I might have.

DEATH. Nope.

STEVE. I was going to get a job though.

DEATH. Nope.

STEVE. Never?

DEATH. Nope.

STEVE. Well, what was I going to do?

DEATH. You were going to sit on that couch and watch TV and play video games for the next fifty years. It doesn't matter though. What might've been is as irrelevant as a single grain of sand beneath the vastness of the ocean. It is time to travel on to your final destination now.

STEVE. Wait. There's one thing I have to know...about the future.

DEATH. Very well. I will answer one question and only one before you move on.

STEVE. What happens on *Lost*[*]? Is the island like purgatory or something?

DEATH. I'm sorry, Steve, but it's never fully explained. Something about magnetic fields, but no one really understands.

STEVE. That's pretty lame. What's going to happen to me now?

DEATH. Well, I'm not really supposed to tell you that. Remaining unbiased is the first rule of reaping souls. But, you look decent enough. A little lazy and pathetic. I suspect your soul will probably wind up in heaven. There's nothing to be afraid of. Have a pleasant journey, Steve.

(DEATH puts his hand on STEVE's head, and they both close their eyes. After a moment STEVE opens his eyes.)

STEVE. I'm still here.

DEATH. That's strange. It could be—no, no, surely that's not it.

STEVE. What is it?

DEATH. Hold on. *(DEATH pulls out a calculator and begins pacing and doing math problems.)* Unfathomable. *(He continues computing.)* This hasn't happened in over 40,000 years.

---

[*] When *Lost* is over, feel free to replace this with a current television program.

STEVE. What? What happened?

DEATH. Apparently, you have achieved a perfect balance upon the scales of good and evil.

STEVE. Is that good?

DEATH. It is neither good nor evil, Steve. It's unfocused and lacking in consistency. It's mediocre to the highest degree.

STEVE. What does it mean?

DEATH. It means that you will be given your choice of final destinations. You will decide whether you are sent to heaven or hell.

STEVE. Heaven.

DEATH. You can't decide yet.

STEVE. Why not?

DEATH. Because your decision will be biased. You have to give both sides a chance to convince you.

STEVE. But then I can pick heaven?

DEATH. If that is your wish. I will go and send for them. You sit in that chair.

(DEATH exits. STEVE stands there for a moment. Then, he sits on the chair and picks up the remote, but before he can turn on the television, there is sudden loud game-show music. Two CREW MEMBERS bring in a wall to separate the chair from the couch. The wall is decorated like the wall in "The Dating Game," but it says "The Fating Game." The two CREW MEMBERS hold up signs to instruct the audience. An ANNOUNCER's voice comes on the loudspeaker.)

ANNOUNCER *(excited)*. Welcome to the game show where chance and circumstance determine your final dance. Time to find out if Steve, a gamer and television connoisseur, will be put to rest with the blessed or the stressed. It's time for... *(The CREW MEMBERS hold up signs that say "The Fating Game." The audience yells with the ANNOUNCER.)* The Fating Game! *(ANNOUNCER by himself.)* Now here's your host, Donnie Destiny!

(DONNIE DESTINY enters. The CREW MEMBERS hold up signs that say "Applause." DONNIE DESTINY is enthusiastic, like all game-show hosts.)

DONNIE DESTINY. Howdy all! Howdy all! I'm Donnie Destiny! You all know how the show works. Our contestant asks questions that the King of Kings and the Dark Lord have to answer, then based on those answers the contestant chooses a fate. You ready Steve?

STEVE. Not really. I don't—

DONNIE DESTINY. Great! Then without further ado let's meet your fates.

ANNOUNCER. Our first fate has been the dark ruler of hell since the dawn of good and evil. You may know him as Beelzebub, Lucifer, or the Prince of Darkness. Let's welcome, from the Hebrew for accuser, Satan.

(SATAN enters and sits on the couch. He waves at the studio audience. The CREW MEMBERS hold up "Applause" signs again.)

DONNIE DESTINY. Good to have you, Satan.

SATAN. It's good to be here, Don.

DONNIE DESTINY. So, the Prince of Darkness, huh?

SATAN. That's right.

DONNIE DESTINY. A job like that must come with one heck of an expense account.

(The CREW MEMBERS hold up signs that read "laughter.")

ANNOUNCER. Fate number two is arriving straight from heaven where he enjoys having his name praised, hymns of thanksgiving and long walks on the clouds. Give it up for notorious G-O-D!

(The CREW MEMBERS hold up signs that read "Hoo! Hoo! Hoo!" GOD glides in and sits next to SATAN.)

DONNIE DESTINY. God, great to have you here!

GOD. Thanks, Donnie. Glad I could come.

DONNIE DESTINY *(looks at his note cards)*. It says here you're the lord and master of all you survey.

GOD. That's right, Donnie.

DONNIE DESTINY. A job like that must come with one heck of an expense account.

(The CREW MEMBERS hold up the "laughter" signs.)

DONNIE DESTINY. All right, now that everyone's present and accounted for, let's play...

(The CREW MEMBERS hold up signs that read "The Fating Game.")

EVERYONE. The Fating Game!

(A CREW PERSON rushes on and hands STEVE the cards with the questions on them. STEVE reads from them.)

STEVE. Fate number one: if you could give me one gift, and it could be anything, what would it be?

SATAN. I'm glad you asked me that, Stevie— I like your voice. It's kind of manly and sexy. I bet you're tall. If I could give you one gift, Stevie, it would be the perfect day. We'd wake up at noon, watch a little *Star Trek*—I love watching guys watch *Star Trek*. We'd eat all the junk food we could get our hands on, and the ice cream would be the kind that doesn't melt so that we wouldn't have to get up and put it away. Then we could smear the ice cream—

GOD. This is disgusting! Really! If I could give you one gift right now Steve, it would be the gift to see this Satan in his true form. I mean, honestly, do you think Satan really sounds like that?

SATAN. What are you talking about? You're such a geek.

DONNIE DESTINY. Now, now. Remember, we aren't supposed to identify each other. We don't want to bias Steve's choice. Am I right, Steve-a-rino?

STEVE. I guess. Fate number two, how much responsibility would you expect of me?

GOD. A great deal, and yet none at the same time. For when you take joy in your responsibility, you will want to be accountable for it.

SATAN *(bursts out laughing)*. I'm sorry. Seriously? A great deal and yet none at the same time. Does that even mean anything? Look Steve, choose me, and if you consider playing video games, and watching TV, and doing

whatever you want whenever you want responsibility—
then you can expect a lot.

GOD. Think of how that worked out for you in life, Steve.
I will help you be a happier more satisfied soul, not en-
able you to destroy yourself. That is why you should
choose me.

SATAN *(getting more angry)*. No, you will choose me,
Steve, because you don't want to be better! You want to
be a disgusting slob who chokes on potato chips!

GOD. You would be wise to choose goodness, Steve.

SATAN *(completly losing it)*. Goodness is for pansies like
you! *(To STEVE.)* You will choose me because I am the
Dark Prince of Hell. You will burn in hellfire, Steve,
and you'll like it. You will come with me and drown in
despair and pain.

DONNIE DESTINY *(still lighthearted)*. Oh no, not again.

*(A "something-bad-happened" game show sound effect
plays.)*

SATAN *(back to sweet)*. Sorry, Donnie.

STEVE. Okay. Um, If I were an ice cream cone, what
would you do with me?

GOD. I would store you at just the right temperature so
you wouldn't ever melt, but you wouldn't lose your
smooth consistency, and—

SATAN *(still livid)*. I would crush you until your soul
melted, and I would let it drip slowly into my mouth.
That's right! I would eat your soul! Then I would drop
the cone on the ground and smash it with my foot. You
will bow before almighty Satan! You insignificant bug!

STEVE. Um, I think I've made my choice.

(Winner sound effects and music play. CREW MEM-BERS hold up "Applause" signs.)

DONNIE DESTINY. Looks like Steve has chosen a fate! Congratulations, Steve! And a huge thanks to all our contestants today. This is Donnie Destiny, and I'll see you next time on…

(CREW holds up "The Fating Game" signs.)

EVERYONE. The Fating Game!

(Everyone begins exiting, and all the "Fating Game" props and set are taken off stage to the theme music. STEVE continues sitting on the couch.)

ANNOUNCER. Contestants not appearing on stage will receive their choice of an eternity in the luxurious clouds of heaven or the fiery pit of hell and a year's supply of Germ-X hand sanitizer. Scrub your sin away with Germ-X.

(Once everyone is gone, DEATH reenters.)

DEATH. Did you make your decision?
STEVE. Yes.
DEATH. Very well, then. *(Begins to exit.)*
STEVE. Where are you going? I've made up my mind.
DEATH. That's good, but now you have to resume your life and earn that choice.
STEVE. I get to live again?
DEATH. For a while, but don't worry, I'll be back soon.

(Blackout.)

SCENE THREE

SETTING: *GOD is sitting at a desk in an office, working.*

AT RISE: *DEATH enters in his classical form, black cloak and scythe. Another portion of the stage serves as Death's home. DEATH is referred to as BILL for the rest of the play.*

BILL. You wanted to see me?

GOD. Yes. Have a seat. *(BILL sits in a chair across from the desk.)* Death, do you know why I asked to see you today?

BILL. No.

GOD. Well, I want to start by sharing with you some of the letters I've been getting. *(GOD opens a drawer of the desk, pulls out a stack of papers and begins reading one.)* "Dear God, all my life I feared death, but now I understand that it was an irrational fear, and a waste of much of my life. I wish I would have known this sooner. This information, together with the meaning of life, which is obviously—" blah...blah...blah. This part gets a little long-winded. Here we go. "When I first awoke and found that my body and soul had been torn from each other, I felt an uncontrollable fear of the unknown path ahead. This fear grew exponentially when the Reaper showed up, but it turned out that Blue Oyster Cult was right. There was no need to fear him. *(BILL slumps in his chair as GOD gives him a quick stern look.)* He sat me down, and he explained to me that everything was going to be okay, and that I was safe. He asked me if I thought I had led a good life, and when I answered yes, he told me that that would be enough to get me into heaven." Here's another. "Dear God, that Reaper of yours is the bomb. I was totally freaked out to be dead and stuff, but he was all, "chill, bro. It'll be all good." I have about a thousand more like this. Do I need to keep going?

BILL. No.

GOD. Let me see if I have this right. You've been telling anyone and everyone who dies that they're going to heaven, and that everything will be okay, and that there's nothing to be afraid of anymore. Is that about right?

BILL. I ask them if they've led a good life first.

GOD. So people are deciding the afterlife for themselves now.

BILL. You don't understand. They're completely hysterical when I show up. If I don't show a little compassion—

GOD. A little compassion! A little compassion? Tell me, what's the number one rule of reaping souls?

BILL. Death can't be biased, but—

GOD. And why must Death remain unbiased?

BILL. Because otherwise people end up in the wrong place.

GOD. And wouldn't you agree that people ending up in the wrong place is a monumental error.

BILL. Yes.

GOD. Or do I need to remind you of the three days after you sent Jesus to hell?

BILL. He told me he was responsible for all the sin in the world! What was I supposed to think.

GOD. That's the point I'm getting at. You are not supposed to be thinking at all. You go by the book. I don't want to go into the bureaucratic nightmare of getting Jesus back. Let's just say I'm not interested in dealing with that problem again.

BILL. I'm sorry. It just started to become painful for me. All this sorting people into Heaven souls or Hell souls. People are scared enough when they've just died. It was easy when I first got started, but as I got older and sorted more souls, I started to realize that Heaven and Hell is a black and white idea. There's no middle ground. Someone who's just a little evil goes to the same place as Hitler? That doesn't make sense. I'm sorry. It got difficult and stressful for me because it's kind of dumb, but I'll go by the book from now on.

GOD. I'm sorry, but, unfortunately, I have no choice but to replace you. You're fired, Bill.

BILL. What! For a little compassion? For trying to do the right thing? I just want people to have a good death. A painless transition from Earth to afterlife.

GOD. I know you do. Unfortunately, that's not the way it works. The afterlife is supposed to be all scary and Biblical. I wish it did work like that, Bill, but it doesn't.

BILL. Surely, you can appreciate the connotations of this outfit. People see it as evil. They're scared of me when they see it. They need to be consoled.

(Another Reaper, JEREMY, enters.)

GOD. I'm going to need you to turn over your scythe to the new Death. *(Indicates the Reaper who just walked in.)*

BILL. What! You gave my job to Jeremy? Jeremy?

JEREMY. The name Jeremy no longer holds any meaning for me. I am…Death.

BILL. No, I am…Death.

JEREMY. No, you're Bill now.

GOD. Death is right, Bill.

BILL. Quit calling Jeremy "Death"! He is not Death! He's not qualified.

JEREMY. Excuse me? Not qualified? I'll have you know that I have been the reaper of insects for over forty million years, and I have taken many a confused bug from the Earth to eternity without passion or prejudice.

BILL. They're bugs! Do you know how many bugs there are on Earth right at this moment! Ten quintillion! That's a one with nineteen zeros! Have you ever stepped on a bug, Jeremy? God? They're freakin' immortal. Where you been, Jeremy? Where you been, huh?

JEREMY. Death needs his scythe, Bill. People need to be able to die. Give me the scythe so I can do my job. I can't be Death without the scythe. Hand it over.

BILL. Okay. Okay. You win. Just give me a few seconds to— Look over there!

(BILL runs from the room as fast as he can and takes the scythe with him. JEREMY and GOD stand silent and awkward for a moment.)

JEREMY. He took the scythe. That can't be good. *(GOD gives him a scathing look.)* I'll go find him.

(JEREMY exits as the lights go down.)

SCENE FOUR

SETTING: *A living room with a door to the outside.*

AT RISE: *BILL enters his home in a panic. He is still dressed in the death cloak. He starts looking for a place to hide the scythe, but they all seem too obvious.*

CONCEPTION *(from offstage)*. Bill, is that you?
BILL. Yes, honey. I'm just—don't come in here.

(He finally hides the scythe under the couch cushions, just as his wife, CONCEPTION, enters. She wears a white cloak.)

CONCEPTION. How was your day at work? What's wrong? You look awfully sad. Did you have a yucky day?

(BILL sits on the couch. He looks very nervous.)

BILL. Conception, I have to tell you something. I— How was your day?
CONCEPTION. It was as wonderful and life affirming as usual. I spread many seeds today and gave life to a great many souls. It's a very fulfilling job, and I feel so blessed, like a bee who has found a flower with very yummy honey, and every day the little bee gets to go eat from that special yummy honey flower. That's how I feel.
BILL. Good. I'm glad you feel like that. That's good.

CONCEPTION. I think somebody needs a great big love hug. Am I right? Here comes the love hug. *(She squeezes him hard and makes a big sigh. She does not let go.)*

BILL. Conception. Conception. I have to tell you something. Do you have a minute?

CONCEPTION. Hold on. Let me check my little schedule. Things always start to get busy when it gets dark out. *(Checks her schedule.)* Well, this is strange. I've never—

BILL. What is it?

CONCEPTION. My schedule is completely empty. I've been Conception for thousands of years, and I've never had an empty schedule before. This scares me, Bill. What's happening out there?

BILL. Don't worry. Everything is fine. It's just that, I did something today. I did something bad.

CONCEPTION. There. There. It can't be all that bad. Just tell me what happened.

BILL. Well, I guess, I—

(BILL tries very hard to say it. He takes some deep breaths. Finally, he picks up the remote control and turns on the TV. The TV ANCHORMAN and STEVE are lit by a spotlight.)

TV ANCHORMAN. Riots are breaking out everywhere! In just a few short minutes, they have become a staple of every major city in the world. Stores and homes are being ravenously looted and decimated as the rioters unite under the ominous chant, "Hooray, hooray, we're invincible." Our in-studio guest today is Reverend Steve. Good evening, Reverend.

STEVE. Good evening, brother.

TV ANCHORMAN. I think what people want to know is, what's going on? Do the rules of death no longer apply?

STEVE. I think the answer is obvious, my brother. The Lord God hath come down from his heavenly throne, and he is testing us. He is testing us like he tested Noah with pain and destruction. Like he tested Job with pain and destruction. Like he tested Master Chief* with pain and destruction—

(BILL turns off the TV and the spotlight disappears.)

BILL. I got fired today.

CONCEPTION. So...there's no more death. They didn't replace you? I mean, I'm sad you lost your job, but...

BILL. Well, they— *(There is a sudden banging on the door. BILL jumps to the floor. CONCEPTION stands up confused.)* Who is it?!

GOD *(off)*. It's the King of Kings! The Lord your God!

SATAN *(off)*. And the Prince of Darkness!

JEREMY *(off)*. And Jeremy. I mean...Death.

BILL. It's not fair! *(BILL pulls the scythe out from the couch cushions.)* I'm holding the scythe right now. If you come in, I'm going to bust it in half! Then no one can ever die again.

GOD. You're going to destroy the world to save yourself, Bill? I thought you knew right from wrong.

_____

* Master Chief is the protagonist of the popular Halo video games. Feel free to replace Master Chief with any video game or television reference.

BILL. I do, but this is the only way. I don't have a choice.

SATAN. Do it, Bill! Break it! What? Oh yeah, Sorry. Don't break it. It would be a totally awesome thing to do, but it really would screw up everything.

GOD. Look, Bill. I know it's hard, and that things don't always makes sense, and that sometimes right and wrong get confusing, but if Satan and I agree on something, don't you think you should listen?

BILL. No!

CONCEPTION. They're right, Bill.

BILL. What? You're my wife! The most ridiculously compassionate, touchy-feely person I know. You're supposed to be defending me.

CONCEPTION. If no one…finishes living, then no new souls can have a turn to experience life. You don't want that. I know you, Bill. You aren't the type to destroy the world. That's not compassion. Give me the scythe, Bill. I know you want to be a good person. Give it to me.

BILL. But, it's everything that I am. Death is my entire existence.

CONCEPTION. Don't be afraid, Bill. This is not the end for you. It's just something new. You're not afraid of something new, are you?

(BILL pauses for a moment. Then he hands the scythe over.)

BILL. It's over. You can come in now.

(The door opens, and GOD, SATAN and JEREMY enter. CONCEPTION gives JEREMY the scythe.)

JEREMY. You are Conception? My new wife? *(CONCEP-TION nods. JEREMY looks at her for a second.)* Nice! *(To BILL.)* Are you ready to come peacefully?

BILL. I—I guess I don't really have a choice.

JEREMY. Don't worry. I'll take good care of her. Or do worry. It makes no difference to me. For I am...Death. *(He takes BILL by the arm.)*

BILL *(scared)*. Jeremy, can you tell me what's—what's going to happen to me, now?

JEREMY. I can tell you what's going to happen to you if you call me Jeremy one more time.

(A classic rock song plays as they exit.)

END OF PLAY

DIRECTOR'S NOTES

DIRECTOR'S NOTES

DIRECTOR'S NOTES

DIRECTOR'S NOTES

DIRECTOR'S NOTES

DIRECTOR'S NOTES